Art and Culture

ORIGAMI

Dividing Fractions

Heather E. Schwartz

Contributing Author

Alison S. Marzocchi, Ph.D.

Consultant

Colleen Pollitt, M.A.Ed.
Math Support Teacher
Howard County Public Schools

Publishing Credits

Rachelle Cracchiolo, M.S.Ed., *Publisher*
Conni Medina, M.A.Ed., *Editor in Chief*
Dona Herweck Rice, *Series Developer*
Emily R. Smith, M.A.Ed., *Series Developer*
Diana Kenney, M.A.Ed., NBCT, *Content Director*
Stacy Monsman, M.A., *Editor*
Michelle Jovin, M.A., *Associate Editor*
Fabiola Sepulveda, *Graphic Designer*

Image Credits: p.22 (right) U.S. Department of Defense; p.22 (bottom) Imperial War Museums, UK; p.23 Yasemin Olgunoz Berber/Shutterstock; all other images from iStock and/or Shutterstock.

Library of Congress Cataloging-in-Publication Data

Names: Schwartz, Heather E., author.
Title: Origami : dividing fractions / Heather E. Schwartz.
Description: Huntington Beach, CA : Teacher Created Materials, [2019] | Series: Art and culture | Includes index. |
Identifiers: LCCN 2018047765 (print) | LCCN 2018052806 (ebook) | ISBN 9781425855215 (eBook) | ISBN 9781425858773 (pbk.)
Subjects: LCSH: Origami--Juvenile literature. | Fractions--Juvenile literature.
Classification: LCC TT872.5 (ebook) | LCC TT872.5 .S39 2019 (print) | DDC 736/.982--dc23
LC record available at https://lccn.loc.gov/2018047765

Teacher Created Materials
5301 Oceanus Drive
Huntington Beach, CA 92649-1030
www.tcmpub.com

ISBN 978-1-4258-5877-3

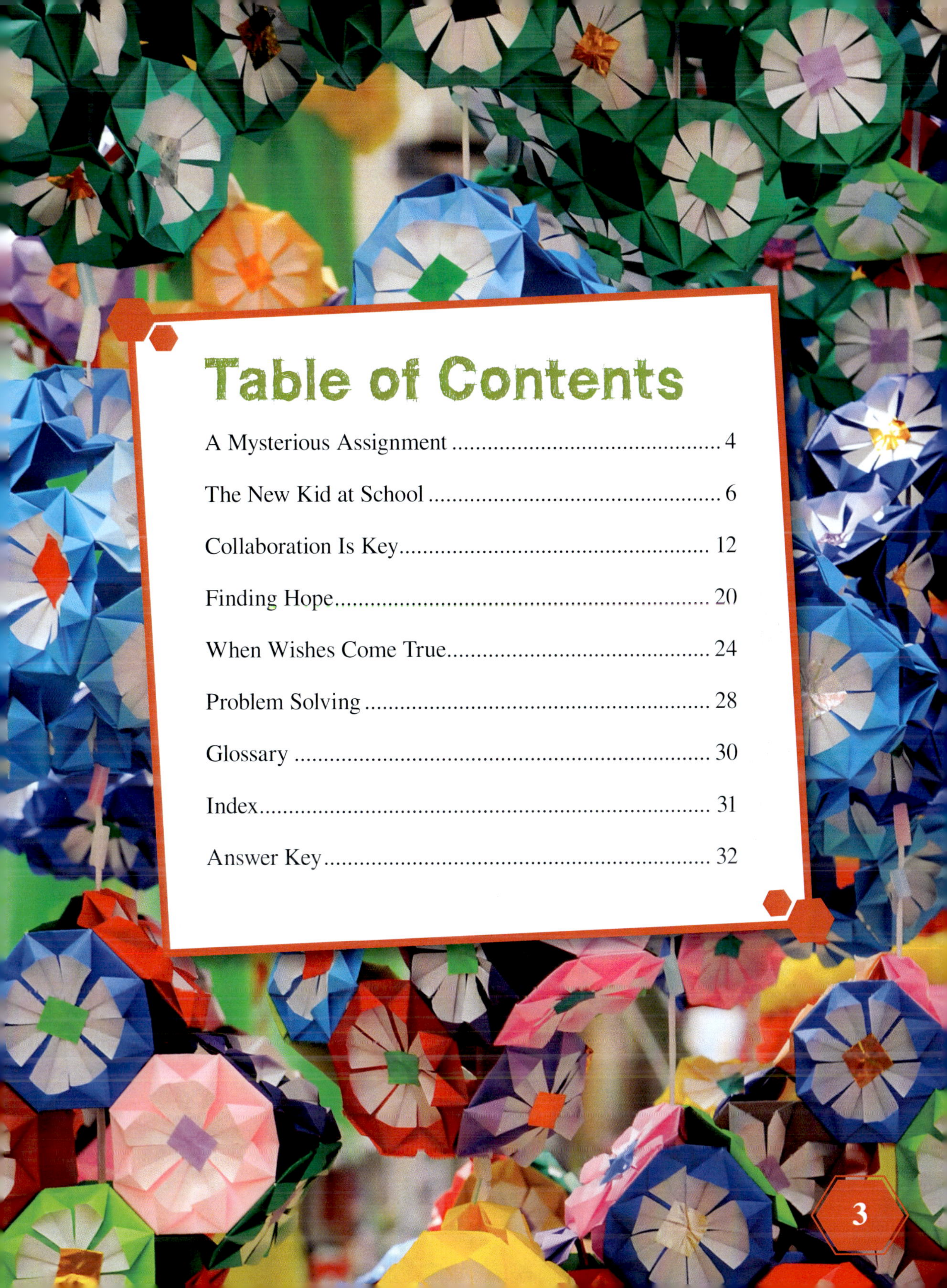

Table of Contents

A Mysterious Assignment

Alexis glanced at the clock. Time was running out; social studies class was almost over. Ms. Diaz surely would have mentioned any homework assignment by now. It wasn't that Alexis minded homework so much, and she even liked social studies. But the textbook was so heavy! She just hated lugging it home.

Suddenly, Ms. Diaz clapped her hands together and stopped the lesson abruptly. "We have to end here," she announced. "I have an important assignment to talk to you about—you'll start work on it this weekend!"

Students listen as Ms. Diaz explains the homework assignment.

Ms. Diaz sounded excited, but Alexis was **skeptical**. Her teacher was probably going to assign the end-of-chapter questions as homework like she did after every unit. And as usual, Ms. Diaz was trying to make it sound more interesting than it really was. Besides, whatever the assignment, it was sure to require carrying that huge textbook home.

Alexis and the rest of the class waited for Ms. Diaz to begin a **prolonged** explanation about the assignment. But their teacher didn't say a word. Instead, she took a sheet of yellow paper from the bin of art supplies and began to fold it carefully on top of her desk.

Ms. Diaz starts folding paper to demonstrate the assignment.

The New Kid at School

As Ms. Diaz folded and creased the paper, she said, "*Origami* means 'to fold paper' in Japanese." She then explained that people can make many different things from a square piece of paper. Everyone laughed when she held up her finished design. It was a paper airplane!

"I thought you said you didn't want any **contraband** in your classroom," called out Kenji, the outspoken new kid. A week earlier, he'd been texting during class, and Ms. Diaz had taken his phone away until after school.

"That's right, I did say that, and I meant it, too," Ms. Diaz **concurred**, her tone stern. "But this is more than just a paper airplane. This is educational."

Alexis groaned inwardly. *Educational*? As she held her pencil above her notepad, waiting to write down the assignment, she couldn't help thinking that this assignment would be boring.

"How can a paper airplane be educational?" Kenji asked, sounding genuinely curious. Alexis noticed Ms. Diaz was letting him get away with not raising his hand. Ms. Diaz wasn't always **stringent** about that particular class rule. It was fine with Alexis, who was curious too, but was shy talking in class.

"That's for you to discover as you work," Ms. Diaz said. "We are learning about cultures from around the world. Your assignment is to work in groups of two and research Japan's culture through origami. Please take your instructions for this assignment from the front of the room as you leave."

LET'S EXPLORE MATH

Ms. Diaz's paper airplane was 8 inches long. Kenji asked to decorate it with different colored stripes. He made each stripe $\frac{1}{4}$-inch wide. Draw an area model like this one. Use it to find out how many stripes Kenji made.

Alexis, Kenji, and the other students stood up and moved to the front of the classroom to pick up the instruction sheet. Alexis looked it over quickly before she put it away in her messenger bag. Their research on origami and Japanese culture needed to be creative and meaningful. Ms. Diaz suggested planning a skit, and Alexis predicted that most kids would do that. She wished there was some way to do the report without feeling so uncomfortable in front of the class. What a **conundrum**!

Ms. Diaz had paired up the students' names in two columns at the bottom of the page. Alexis scanned the pairings, looking for her name. There it was—she was paired with Kenji.

Remembering how talkative Kenji had been in class, Alexis hoped he wasn't a troublemaker. As she was walking toward the door, she glanced toward Kenji's desk and saw that he was sitting down instead of getting ready to leave like everyone else. He'd torn a sheet of paper out of his notebook and was busy folding it into different shapes. *Another paper airplane? What was he up to?* Alexis wondered.

Kenji folds a paper airplane before going to art class.

Alexis gets ready to leave Ms. Diaz's room to go to art class.

Kenji Remembers

In art class, Kenji painted his clay sculpture, following the teacher's instructions. Even though he was in art class, his mind was on the origami assignment. He thought back to the night his grandmother told him a story about origami.

As Kenji paints, his mind is on origami and his grandmother's story.

LET'S EXPLORE MATH

As Kenji's grandmother folded paper cranes, it took her $\frac{1}{2}$ minute to make each one.

1. Draw a number line like this one. Use it to find out how many paper cranes Kenji's grandmother made in 12 minutes.

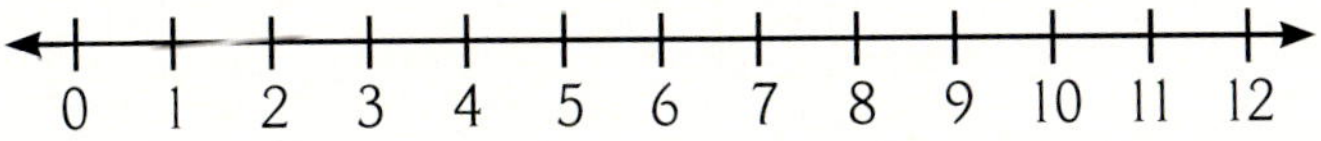

2. Which expression can be used to find the total number of cranes Kenji's grandmother made? Explain the reasoning for your choice.

   A. $12 \times \frac{1}{2}$

   B. $12 \div \frac{1}{2}$

   C. $\frac{1}{2} \div 12$

"In Japan, we say that those who fold 1,000 paper cranes will be granted a wish," his grandmother had said, taking a square piece of orange paper out of a box. "When I was a student many years ago, a girl named Sadako Sasaki (suh-DAH-koh sah-SAH-kee) set out to achieve this goal. But she was very ill. She only managed to make 644 cranes."

Kenji had reached for a piece of paper to try for himself and began folding quickly, without watching how his grandmother did it.

"This is a squash fold," she explained patiently as she noticed Kenji's mistakes. She reached for his paper and said, "Here, let me show you."

Kenji remembered how frustrated he felt as he crumpled his piece of paper, much to his grandmother's **chagrin**.

Back in class, Kenji tried to remember the shape of the finished paper crane his grandmother had called a symbol of peace and hope. He couldn't help but wonder whether Sadako had friends who could have helped her make more paper cranes. Maybe she was like him—lonely and friendless.

Collaboration Is Key

On Saturday, Alexis and Kenji made plans to meet at noon at the county library. Alexis waved good-bye to her mother and hurried up the steps to the library. She was early but wanted to **strategize** on her own before Kenji got there. That way, they wouldn't **squander** their time together.

A quick search on the computer provided a lot of basic information about origami. Alexis jotted down a few **relevant** facts in her notebook.

> *Origami is an art form that is also called paper folding.*
> *It started in either China or Japan thousands of years ago.*

She found one website that described the different folds used in origami. The mountain and valley folds looked easy enough. Alexis liked the names of some of the others, such as the rabbit ear fold and the petal fold. She tore a piece of paper out of her notebook and tried to make a small paper box by reading an origami diagram. Lines, dashes, and other symbols showed which kinds of folds to make.

Struggling to **decipher** the directions, Alexis quickly abandoned her effort. The finished box in the illustration looked cute, but she needed more facts for their report. As she typed in another search, a loud bang disrupted the quiet room. Her head swiveled toward the sound.

Alexis starts her research on origami.

LET'S EXPLORE MATH

Alexis noticed directions for an origami creation that started with folding and unfolding square paper in half four different ways. She saw that this divided the square into eight triangles.

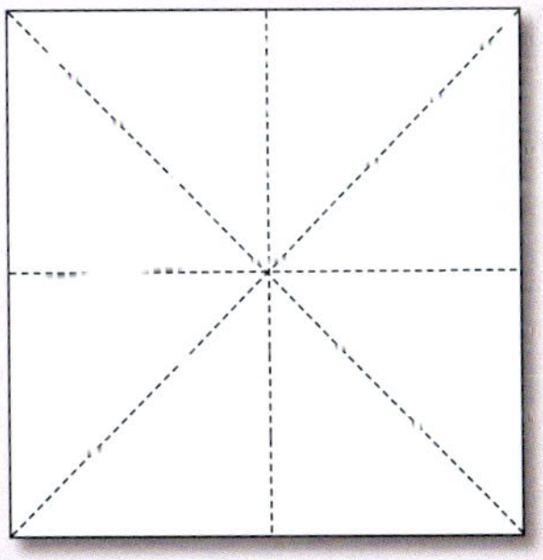

1. What fraction of the square does each triangle represent? How do you know?
2. While practicing this creation, Alexis folded 5 sheets of origami paper in this way. How many total triangles did she form? Write and solve multiplication and division equations to show your thinking.
3. How are the equations related?

Near the front door, Kenji righted a rack of books he'd knocked over when he'd sprinted into the library. "Sorry!" he apologized to the librarian.

"Don't worry, it's not a catastrophe," the librarian said, her own voice **muted**. "Just be careful and speak quietly while you're here."

Spotting Alexis at the computer, he trotted over and unzipped his backpack. "I made all these last night!" he whispered.

Peering in, Alexis saw many paper airplanes in different colors and styles. "Wow," she whispered back, impressed.

"I used special origami paper my grandmother brought from Japan," Kenji told her. "She gave me a bunch of sheets—see how the paper is square, not a rectangle like regular paper." Kenji pulled out the origami paper from his backpack.

Alexis added these notes in her notebook. "Do you want to show these paper airplanes when we give our report?" she asked.

"No, these paper airplanes will be the whole report!" Kenji said, more loudly. "We'll race them and measure **velocity**!"

Alexis looked **dubious**. "But this is a social studies project, not math or science," she said, turning back to the computer screen. "Maybe we could make other things out of origami. What about paper boats?"

Kenji shook his head. "Ms. Diaz said we have to make something meaningful and creative," he said. "Paper airplanes meet both requirements. What's the point of making boats or anything else?"

Kenji shows Alexis the paper airplanes he folded.

LET'S EXPLORE MATH

Kenji made some small paper airplanes to show Alexis. He started with $\frac{1}{4}$ square of origami paper. Then, he cut that into 4 smaller squares to make the airplanes.

1. What fraction of the whole square is each small paper airplane? Use the diagram to find your answer.
2. Write and solve a division equation to show your thinking.

Alexis thought the point was obvious, but she replied anyway. "Boats and other things would show the class different examples of origami," she said. "We could put some on the desk like decorations while we read our report."

Kenji sat next to Alexis and took a piece of origami paper. He folded it about one-half inch (about one centimeter) and flipped it over. He folded the paper again, lining up the edges. Kenji repeated the two steps until the whole sheet was contained in one thin strip. He pinched it together at the top and bottom, then let go of the top and watched it spring open into a fan.

Kenji displays his fan while Alexis thinks of ways to make the report interesting.

"Too bad it's winter here," he said, recalling the year-round warm weather in his hometown. "If it was hot, we could make these cool fans for the whole class—and then they'd be fans of us!"

Alexis smiled at the **pun** but reminded him, "Well, the only person we have to impress is Ms. Diaz since she's the one giving out the grades."

"Still, the report has to be creative," Kenji **mused**. "Maybe we should act it out, otherwise everyone will fall asleep."

Alexis knew that Kenji was right. "I hate speaking in front of the class," she blurted out. "I wish we could think of something else." But she didn't have any other brilliant ideas.

Alexis and Kenji's voices had grown louder as they discussed their project, and they caught the librarian's attention. She was soon at their table.

"Perhaps you kids would like to use one of our meeting rooms if you need to talk a lot," she suggested.

Alexis stood up to move, but Kenji was feeling restless in the library. "Let's walk to my house—it's really close, and you can meet my grandmother. She might be able to help us come up with an idea since she knows a lot about origami," he said.

Alexis texted her mom to ask if she could go to Kenji's house. Her mom said it was fine and that she would pick Alexis up there later. As they left the library, Kenji opened his bag again. "Now we can fly these," he said, handing Alexis a brown plane and taking a green one for himself.

"These are really cool shapes," Alexis said enthusiastically.

"Yeah, the brown one is called a bottlenose because of the tip on the end. And the other one is called a tailed plane," Kenji answered, adding, "I have a book about making paper airplanes."

All the way to Kenji's house, they pulled the rest of the paper planes from his bag and raced them, guessing which ones would win. When they reached his front door, they were both laughing and out of breath.

LET'S EXPLORE MATH

Kenji's house is $1\frac{1}{3}$ blocks away from the library. His paper airplane traveled $\frac{1}{6}$ of a block each time he threw it.

1. How many times did Kenji throw his paper airplane walking from the library to his house? Draw and use a number line like this one to solve the problem.

2. Which question does your work on the number line help you answer?

   A. How many $\frac{1}{6}$ make $1\frac{1}{3}$?

   B. How many $1\frac{1}{3}$ make $\frac{1}{6}$?

   C. What is $\frac{1}{6}$ of $1\frac{1}{3}$?

   D. What is $\frac{1}{6}$ more than $1\frac{1}{3}$?

Finding Hope

Kenji's grandmother greeted them with a smile and a question. "Is this your new friend whom you met at the library?" she asked Kenji.

"Um, this is Alexis," he answered, avoiding his classmate's eyes. "We're working together on a project about origami." They'd had fun on the walk over, but it seemed too soon to use the word *friend*. He wished it wasn't, but he was the new kid at school. Alexis already had friends. Kenji was a little embarrassed.

Kenji's grandmother told them to sit at the kitchen table, and she brought out a plate of cookies for them.

Kenji's grandmother folds cranes as she tells the story.

"Did you tell Alexis about Sadako Sasaki? How her classmates got together and helped her finish her one thousand paper cranes?" his grandmother asked. "And I was honored to be one of them."

Kenji looked up, with renewed interest. "I don't remember the whole story. That's why I invited Alexis home to meet you," he said.

"Once you know how, paper cranes are not difficult to make," she said as she began folding. "I can teach you, while I tell you both about my friend Sadako."

Alexis pulled out her notebook, ready to write the points she wanted to include in their presentation. Kenji's grandmother asked him for a piece of origami paper. She placed it on the table. Then, she started to fold as she spoke.

LET'S EXPLORE MATH

Kenji's grandmother used all her sugar to make the cookies. She had $2\frac{1}{2}$ cups of sugar. One batch of cookies needed $\frac{3}{4}$ cup of sugar.

1. Did Kenji's grandmother make more than, less than, or exactly 1 batch of cookies? How do you know?
2. Kenji wants to find out how many batches of cookies she made. His work is shown. Do you agree with Kenji's thinking and solution? Why or why not?

$$\frac{3}{4} \div 2\frac{1}{2}$$

$$\frac{3}{4} \div \frac{5}{2}$$

$$\frac{3}{4} \times \frac{2}{5} = \frac{6}{20} = \frac{3}{10}$$

$\frac{3}{10}$ of a batch

At first, Alexis and Kenji just watched and listened. After Kenji's grandmother finished making a paper crane, they wanted to try too. Kenji handed Alexis a piece of origami paper, then took one for himself.

His grandmother showed them how to fold the bird base first, to create the crane's body. This time, Kenji paid close attention, following her folds step-by-step.

While they worked, Kenji's grandmother told them more about Sadako. "She developed a form of cancer called leukemia (loo-KEE-mee-ah) as a result of the atomic bomb dropped on Hiroshima (heh-ROH-sheh-muh) during World War II," she explained. "Sadako's cancer had no cure, but she had hope. She made a wish that if she folded a thousand paper cranes, she would be well again."

The atomic bomb destroyed Hiroshima on August 6, 1945.

"Did her wish come true?" Alexis asked.

Knowing the answer, Kenji shook his head as his grandmother continued. "The story has a sad ending but a hopeful ending too," she said. "Sadako did not recover, but her life inspired people to make the world a more peaceful place. A place without bombs and without war."

They finished their paper cranes and held them up. "Another start toward one thousand paper cranes!" Kenji's grandmother declared happily.

And suddenly, Kenji knew exactly how he and Alexis should do their report.

The Children's Peace Monument in Hiroshima commemorates Sadako Sasaki and other child victims of the atomic bombing.

When Wishes Come True

On the day of their presentation, Kenji was waiting for Alexis in front of the school. When she arrived, he opened his backpack. “I couldn’t finish,” he said, showing her the paper cranes inside. “I guess it wasn’t such a great idea, thinking we could make 644 cranes by today.”

“It was a great idea, just too ambitious! I couldn’t make my half either,” Alexis said, adding Kenji’s cranes to the ones she carried in a paper bag.

They filed into their classroom together and settled in for math. All through the math lesson, Kenji couldn’t concentrate because he wanted to fold more paper cranes. He even tried to fold one inside his desk where the teacher couldn’t see. But it was impossible because he couldn’t see the paper either. Alexis laughed at his attempts and whispered for him to stop.

Finally, it was time for the first pair’s origami report. Alexis wasn’t surprised when her classmates started acting out a skit they’d written, but while she watched, she suddenly realized she wasn’t nervous about her turn in front of the class. She was actually looking forward to it! She looked over at Kenji and smiled, and he smiled back. When the skit was over, the class applauded, and Ms. Diaz called, “Kenji and Alexis, you can go next.”

Alexis sat at the head of the class folding paper while Kenji spoke, telling them Sadako's story and his grandmother's part in it. He also told the class about the Children's Peace Monument in Hiroshima, Japan. Children from all over the world send more than 10 million cranes every year in her honor.

"It's a symbol of a wish for world peace that Sadako inspired," he explained.

Kenji and Alexis give their presentation.

At that cue, Alexis stood confidently and held up the paper crane she'd folded while Kenji spoke. Now that he'd done most of the talking, she felt ready. Plus, he'd taken all the difficult facts for himself and given her the easy part. She took the class step-by-step through the directions on how to fold a paper crane.

"We tried to fold 644 by today," she said toward the end of their presentation. "We wanted to show you the same number Sadako had folded, but we didn't even get close to our goal."

"We still want to try to fold 1,000 by the end of the year," she continued. "Then, we can send them to the monument."

Ms. Diaz held up her paper crane. "That's a wonderful idea!" she exclaimed. "It will be a class project with all of us working together."

That was their plan all along! Kenji and Alexis looked at each other and smiled. Their presentation may have been over, but their friendship was just beginning.

Problem Solving

At the end of the school year, Ms. Diaz's class meets their goal of folding 1,000 origami cranes. They want to ship the cranes to the Children's Peace Monument in Japan, but the cranes will not fit into one box. Alexis and Kenji have different ideas about the best way to ship the cranes. Alexis wants to use 3 same-sized boxes. Kenji can bring as many boxes as the class needs, but his boxes can only hold $\frac{1}{4}$ pound each. Ms. Diaz tells them that the other students in class will cast votes to choose the shipping plan and explain the reasoning for their choices.

Imagine that you are a member of Ms. Diaz's class. Whose shipping plan would you choose—Alexis's or Kenji's? Be sure to include the following information when casting your vote:

- the number of boxes in the shipment
- the weight of each box
- the reasons the plan you chose is better than the other option

Data from Ms. Diaz:

The total weight of the cranes is $1\frac{4}{5}$ pounds.

Kenji's Plan:

same-sized boxes that each hold $\frac{1}{4}$ pound

Alexis's Plan:

3 same-sized boxes

Glossary

chagrin—frustration

concurred—agreed with someone

contraband—things that are not allowed in a place

conundrum—a very difficult problem

decipher—to figure something out

dubious—unsure about something

mused—thought about something thoroughly

muted—quieter than a usual volume

prolonged—lasting for a long time

pun—a funny way to express something so that more than one meaning can be inferred

relevant—significant or important

skeptical—feeling doubtful about something

squander—to do or use something in a wasteful way

strategize—to make a plan to help meet a goal

stringent—very severe or strict

velocity—how fast someone or something moves

Index

Answer Key

Let's Explore Math

page 7

32 stripes;

page 11

1. 24 cranes;

2. B; Reasoning may include that the expression finds how many $\frac{1}{2}$ minutes make 12 minutes.

page 13

1. $\frac{1}{8}$; There are 8 same-sized triangles formed by the folds.
2. 40 triangles; $5 \times 8 = 40$; $5 \div \frac{1}{8} = 40$
3. The multiplication equation shows 5 groups of 8. The division equation shows how many $\frac{1}{8}$s make 5. Both equations can be solved to show that 40 triangles are formed.

page 15

1. $\frac{1}{16}$
2. $\frac{1}{4} \div 4 = \frac{1}{16}$

page 19

1. 8 times;

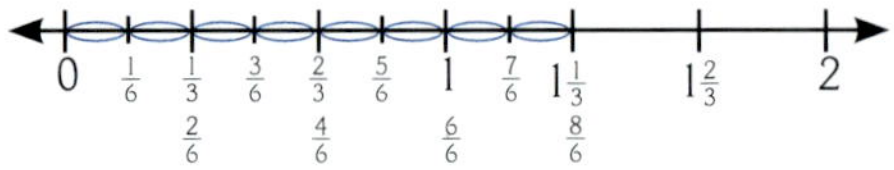

2. A

page 21

1. more than 1 batch of cookies; Each batch needed $\frac{3}{4}$ cup sugar, and Kenji's grandmother used $2\frac{1}{2}$ cups. There is more than one $\frac{3}{4}$ in $2\frac{1}{2}$.
2. disagree; Kenji should have divided $2\frac{1}{2}$ by $\frac{3}{4}$. He needs to find how many $\frac{3}{4}$s are in $2\frac{1}{2}$, not how many $2\frac{1}{2}$s are in $\frac{3}{4}$. Kenji's grandmother made $3\frac{2}{6}$, or $3\frac{1}{3}$, batches of cookies because $2\frac{1}{2} \div \frac{3}{4} = \frac{20}{6} = 3\frac{2}{6} = 3\frac{1}{3}$.

Problem Solving

Votes and reasoning will vary. Examples: *I chose Alexis's plan because it only uses 3 boxes instead of 8. Each box weighs $\frac{9}{15}$, or $\frac{3}{5}$ pound because $1\frac{4}{5} \div 3 = \frac{9}{15}$, or $\frac{3}{5}$.* Or, *I chose Kenji's plan because each box would only weigh $\frac{1}{4}$ pound instead of $\frac{3}{5}$ pound. Using Kenji's plan, it will take 8 boxes instead of 3 because $1\frac{4}{5} \div \frac{1}{4} = \frac{36}{5}$, or $7\frac{1}{5}$. So 7 boxes are not enough to fit all the cranes; 8 are needed.*